50 SPORTS STEM LABS

SPORTS-THEMED STEM & STEAM PROJECTS

FIRST EDITION

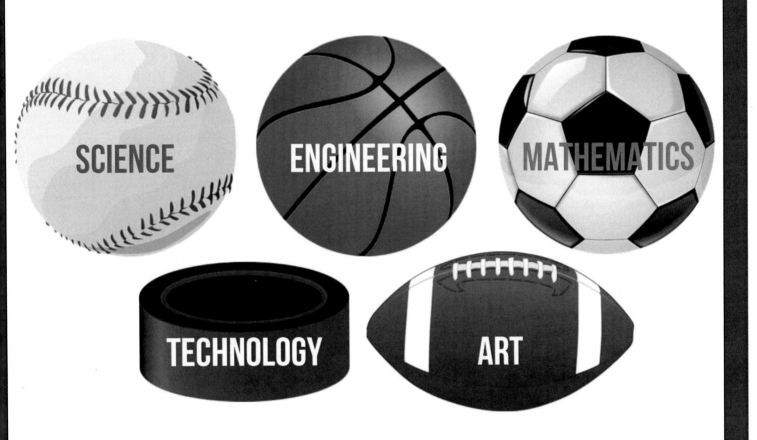

SCIENCE

ENGINEERING

MATHEMATICS

TECHNOLOGY

ART

(C) 2018 ANDREW FRINKLE & MEDIASTREAM PRESS

IN THIS VOLUME:

TABLE OF CONTENTS:

WHAT ARE STEM AND STEAM?

STEM is an acronym for Science, Technology, Engineering, and Mathematics. All of the labs within this volume promote learning within these four fields. You might also find the acronym **STEAM** being used. STEAM is the addition of Art to the other four STEM fields. This book takes a unique route of presenting projects that all deal with team sports, focusing on the popular sports of baseball, basketball, football, ice hockey, and soccer! Learn more at www.50STEMLabs.com.

COPYRIGHT INFORMATION:

All materials and designs contained within this volume are protected by copyright laws and are the property of Andrew Frinkle & MediaStream Press (C) 2018, with the exception of the graphics, which are from public domain sites, primarily www.pixabay.com or www.openclipart.org.

The materials within may only be reproduced for your classroom or at home for educational use. These materials may not be resold for any reason. They may not be hosted on public databases or websites for any reason. For questions & comments, please contact me at: www.MediaStreamPress.com

HOW TO USE THIS BOOK:

GENERAL SUGGESTIONS:

This book contains 50 different STEM lab activities presented as elements of popular team sports. You will find a strong emphasis on designing a project, testing it, measuring the results, and reflecting upon what worked and did not work, which might lead to a redesign and retesting process. Technology can easily be incorporated by recording and documenting the process and creating reports and projects about the topic(s) afterward. Create videos, presentations, blogs, and more to keep track of your experiences. Presentation and sharing of results is key to cooperative learning. Journals and log books should be kept as a record of the learning process.

There are some general suggestions and guidelines for each project, but it has deliberately been left without too much detail to allow the projects to be adapted to your classroom's individual needs. These are not exact step-by-step recipes to follow to make a project or activity. These projects require critical thinking and problem-solving skills.

There is no intended order to these projects, nor is it expected that you will do each project. It is highly recommended that you pick the ones you find to be most interesting or appropriate for each learning group, which might have to be slightly modified, depending on the learning and experience levels you are working with.

You will find some similar projects within this volume and in the additional volumes of the 50 STEM Labs Series. Attempting similar projects helps students build on previous learning experiences while making them adjust to new expectations and rules or materials in the new project. Many instructors have great success with thematic units or quarterly units on bridges, towers, or other sets of related projects. In this case, it would be on specific sports.

Another key part of this series is the idea that learning science should not break the bank. Most projects are done with common and inexpensive school supplies, office supplies, or household objects. Students can even scavenge and recycle supplies for some projects.

Since these events and projects are based on popular team sports, watching and studying the rules and general ideas behind each game is strongly suggested. You might also find ways to modify the labs in this book to make them work for other sports or topics that were not featured within this volume. Be creative and have fun!

BASEBALL STEM LABS

01 ALL STITCHED UP
Create your own custom baseball.

02 BIG GREEN MONSTER
Design your own baseball park.

03 CATCH IT
Create a model catcher that can catch a ball.

04 GEAR UP
Create protective gear for a baseball player.

05 GOLDEN GLOVES
Create your own custom baseball glove.

06 HICKORY STICKS
Create your own custom baseball bat.

07 HOME RUN DERBY
Create a model batter that can hit a ball.

08 HOME TEAM JERSEYS
Create your own custom baseball jersey.

09 NO HITTER
Create a model pitcher that can throw a ball.

10 STEALING FIRST
Create a model base runner that can slide into a base.

 MediaStream Press

BASKETBALL STEM LABS

01 BOUNCE PASS

Build a model player that can bounce a ball and another that can catch it.

02 BRACKETS

Devise an infographic to hold all the information for a tournament.

03 FAST BREAK

Make a series of players that can pass a ball forward toward a hoop and shoot it.

04 HOME COURT ADVANTAGE

Design your own basketball court or arena.

05 HOOP DRILLS

Build a model player that can accurately shoot a ball into a hoop.

06 HOOP IT UP

Design your own basketball hoop and rim.

07 JERSEY CITY

Design your own basketball jersey.

08 NEW KICKS

Design your own basketball shoes.

09 ROBOTS CAN JUMP

Build a model player that can jump as high as possible.

10 SHOT BLOCKERS

Build a model player that can block an opponent's shot.

 (C) 2018 MediaStream Press

FOOTBALL STEM LABS

01 FAIR CATCH

Create a model punt returner that can catch a falling ball.

02 FIELD GOAL KICKERS

Create a model kicker that can kick a stationary ball through uprights.

03 HAIL MARY

Create a model quarterback that can throw a ball as far as possible.

04 MODEL PLAYER

Design safety equipment for a football player.

05 PASS RUSH

Create a model player that can push through an offensive line and hit the quarterback.

06 PIGSKINS

Design a custom football.

07 TACKLED!

Create a model player that can tackle a moving player.

08 TOUCHDOWN!

Create a model player that can push through a defensive line and make it to the end zone.

09 VIBRATING FOOTBALL

Design a vibrating football toy game.

10 WIDE RECEIVER

Create a model receiver that can catch a thrown ball.

 MediaStream Press

ICE HOCKEY STEM LABS

01 BLADES OF STEEL

Design your own pair of hockey skates.

02 BODY CHECK

Create a model player that can knock over an opponent.

03 FRESH JERSEYS

Design your own hockey jersey.

04 GOALIES

Create a model goalie that can protect the net from pucks.

05 HIT THE ICE

Create a model hockey player that can move and shoot a puck.

06 PUCK TIME

Design and test your own hockey puck.

07 RINKY DINK

Design your own model hockey arena or rink.

08 SLAPSHOTS

Create a model hockey player that can shoot a puck as fast or as far as possible.

09 STICK TO THE GAME

Design and test your own hockey stick.

10 SUIT UP

Design safety equipment for an ice hockey player.

MediaStream Press

SOCCER STEM LABS

01 CHECK OUT THIS BALL

Design and test your own soccer ball.

02 CORNER KICKERS

Create a model soccer player that can kick a ball over a to score in a goal.

03 FRESH KITS

Design and test your own soccer uniforms.

04 GOAL CELEBRATIONS

Design and showcase your own goal celebration.

05 ON THE PITCH

Design your own custom soccer pitch.

06 PENALTY KICKERS

Create a model soccer player that can kick a penalty a against a goalkeeper.

07 SHOW STOPPERS

Create a model soccer goalkeeper that can stop incoming shots.

08 SLIDERS

Create a model soccer player that can slide to steal the ball from another player.

09 TABLE SOCCER TIME

Design a working table soccer toy game.

10 TIME TO CLEAT

Design your own custom soccer cleats.

(C) 2018 MediaStream Press

50 SPORTS STEM LABS

STEM & STEAM PROJECTS

EACH OF THE 50 PROJECTS CONTAINS:

- PROJECT TITLE WITH TOPIC TAGS

- PROJECT DETAILS AND EXPLANATIONS

- PROJECT RULES, GUIDELINES, & EXPECTATIONS

- SUGGESTED MATERIALS

- SCORING & GRADING SUGGESTIONS

BASEBALL

BASEBALL-THEMED SPORTS PROJECTS

INSTRUCTOR NOTES:

SOME OF THESE PROJECTS REQUIRE YOU TO BUILD PARTS OF A MODEL BASEBALL FIELD. BUILDING THEM MAY BE TIME AND MATERIAL INTENSIVE. PLAN AHEAD AND SHOP AROUND FOR MATERIALS AND PIECES THAT MAKE THE PROJECT EASIER AND MORE AFFORDABLE.

BASEBALL: ALL STITCHED UP

You can't play baseball without a ball. Get busy making your own. Make sure to experiment with the coatings, weight, and composition to get the best effect.

MISSION RULES AND RESTRICTIONS:

1. Create a model baseball.

2. Your baseball should be near regulation size of 8 inches in circumference and 3 inches in diameter, as well as 5 ounces in weight and should be spherical.

3. The model will be thrown at a target or used in a game of catch.

4. Experiment with coatings and core materials to create specific pitching effects.

5. You will get several attempts to throw your ball. Tests may include ease of catching, accuracy, or other goals, as specified by your instructor.

GRADED ASSIGNMENT SUGGESTIONS:

Grading suggestions include:

- a write-up of ideas, including blueprints

- grade results based upon if the ball actually works, and, if so, how successfully?

- a report on baseballs

- a project advertising a modified baseball with some new feature(s) to make the game different

MATERIALS:

INSTRUCTOR MATERIALS:

- a place to toss a ball

- baseball gloves

- tape measure

- scale

PARTICIPANT MATERIALS:

- real baseballs for comparison

- clay

- tape

- plastic wrap

- tin foil

- cloth

- metal weights

- other approved materials, especially as coverings or core materials for the baseball

STANDARDS: FORCES, FRICTION, MOTION

BASEBALL: BIG GREEN MONSTER

Baseball fields all have their own styles. Some are pretty famous with unique details, like the Big Green Monster in Fenway Park. Design your own baseball park!

MISSION RULES AND RESTRICTIONS:

1. Research the design of a baseball park, paying special attention to the lines and zones of the rink. Include research on how the game is played around those areas, such as the foul lines, infield, dugout positions, outfield walls, etc...

2. Redesign baseball play, adding several new rules and modifications to the classic design of the lines and zones of the field. Position of lines, changes of dimensions, or added areas are some possible alterations.

3. Present your idea (with a model if possible).

4. If possible, play a game on a modified field (even indoor style). This may be reserved for the game modification chosen as the best of the group.

GRADED ASSIGNMENT SUGGESTIONS:

Grading suggestions include:

- a write-up of ideas, including blueprints

- grade results based upon if the design actually works, and, if so, how successfully?

- a report on a baseball field, surfaces and construction, or on the history of baseball field designs and rules

MATERIALS:

INSTRUCTOR MATERIALS:

- an actual baseball field if possible, or pictures of a real field

PARTICIPANT MATERIALS:

- poster board
- white melamine board
- access to printers
- colored tapes
- white tape and markers
- green felt or fake turf carpet
- sandpaper or sand
- markers
- netting
- paint
- plastic straws
- foam sheeting
- cardboard

STANDARDS: DESIGN, MEASUREMENT, MODELS

BASEBALL: CATCH IT

Without a catcher, baseball would be a strange game. Who would return the balls that batters didn't swing at? Who would guard home plate? Make your own catcher model and practice catching pitches!

MISSION RULES AND RESTRICTIONS:

1. Create a baseball player model of a specified size and/or weight, which should include a catcher's mitt and catcher's gear.

2. The model will have to be controlled in front of home plate using a method of your choosing, which may include: puppetry, wind power, magnets, or another approved method.

3. The baseball player will have to catch a ball about the size of a gum ball.

4. The ball should be 'thrown' in a relatively consistent speed and location (the strike zone), possibly through a straw or firing mechanism.

5. You will get 3 to 10 pitches to catch (multiple rounds may be required). If your catcher fails to catch the ball or drops it after catching it, it is considered a failure.

GRADED ASSIGNMENT SUGGESTIONS:

Grading suggestions include:

• a write-up of ideas, including blueprints

• grade results based upon the execution of the model and how accurately it reflects the proposed ideas

• a project about a specific catcher or the history of the catcher position and equipment

MATERIALS:

INSTRUCTOR MATERIALS:

• Model baseball diamond or flat surface (a smooth table, a floor, or sheet of melamine to make your diamond on). Decorate your diamond with at least home plate and a pitcher's mound.

• Scale models of baseball

• Accurate pitching or throwing device

PARTICIPANT MATERIALS:

• paper clips

• notecards

• scissors

• plastic straws

• tape and glue

• popsicle sticks

• foam

• brass fasteners

• string

• other approved materials

STANDARDS: ACCURACY, FORCES, MOTION

BASEBALL: GEAR UP

Baseball usually focuses on protective equipment for the batter, catcher, and the umpire. Sometimes a pitcher wears protective gear in softball, as well. Research the protective gear a baseball player wears, and make modifications to them to change how the sport is played!

MISSION RULES AND RESTRICTIONS:

1. Research baseball catcher gear, helmets, and other protective gear.
2. Use your research to help you design the perfect baseball protective gear.
3. Create a model of your safety equipment.
4. Also create an advertising scheme or sales pitch to present to your peers. Your presentation might include a pitch for a city that does not currently have a team.

MATERIALS:

INSTRUCTOR MATERIALS:

- student access to internet for research
- equipment samples
- Optionally, miniature models or mannikins to place equipment on.

PARTICIPANT MATERIALS:

- fabric, including athletic fabrics
- tape and glue
- colored tape
- paint
- Sewing and design materials
- Scissors
- foam sheeting
- clay
- Other approved, scavenged materials

GRADED ASSIGNMENT SUGGESTIONS:

Grading suggestions include:

- a write-up of ideas, including blueprints
- grade results based upon the practicality of the design and the effectiveness of the sales pitch
- a report on a baseball safety equipment as it has changed over time

STANDARDS: DESIGN, MATERIALS, MODELS

BASEBALL: GOLDEN GLOVES

You can't play baseball without a glove. There are actually several types of gloves, depending on the position you play or if you're right or left-handed. Design a new and unique glove!

MISSION RULES AND RESTRICTIONS:

1. Research baseball gloves, as well as gloves in other sports.
2. Use your research to help you design the perfect baseball glove.
3. Create a model of your glove idea.
4. Test the glove if possible.
5. Also create an advertising scheme or sales pitch to present to your peers.

GRADED ASSIGNMENT SUGGESTIONS:

Grading suggestions include:

- a write-up of ideas, including blueprints
- grade results based upon the execution of the model and how accurately it reflects the proposed ideas
- a report on baseball gloves or a brand of gloves
- a project about hands or the muscles and bones of the hand

MATERIALS:

INSTRUCTOR MATERIALS:

- student access to internet for research
- actual baseball gloves for comparison

PARTICIPANT MATERIALS:

- fabric, including heavier fabrics, leather, and rubber-type materials
- tape and glue
- rubber bands
- colored tape
- cords and string
- paint
- eyelets and shoelaces
- sewing and design materials
- scissors
- other approved, scavenged materials

STANDARDS: ANATOMY, DESIGN, ERGONOMICS, MATERIALS, MODELS

BASEBALL: HICKORY STICKS

You can't play baseball without a bat. Design a model bat of your own!

MISSION RULES AND RESTRICTIONS:

1. Research baseball bats and how they are made.
2. Use your research to help you design the perfect baseball bat.
3. Create a model of your baseball bat idea.
4. Also create an advertising scheme or sales pitch to present to your peers.
5. Optionally, test the baseball bat out if it is of a playable size.

MATERIALS:

INSTRUCTOR MATERIALS:

- student access to internet for research
- baseball bat examples
- optionally, models of players to put the bats next to

PARTICIPANT MATERIALS:

- tape and glue
- colored tapes
- paint
- wood, especially dowel rods, balsa wood and popsicle sticks
- cutting tools
- sandpaper
- access to printing for designs, logos, and letters
- other approved, scavenged materials

GRADED ASSIGNMENT SUGGESTIONS:

Grading suggestions include:

- a write-up of ideas, including blueprints
- grade results based upon the execution of the model and how accurately it reflects the proposed ideas
- a project about baseball bats, the history of baseball bats, or infographics about the brands of baseball bats and their prevalence

STANDARDS: DESIGN, MATERIALS, MODELS

BASEBALL: HOME RUN DERBY

Hearing the crack of the bat is probably the most exciting part of baseball. You're always looking for that base on ball or one of those long fly balls that either gets caught or goes over the fence. Design a home run hitting machine!

MISSION RULES AND RESTRICTIONS:

1. Create a baseball player model of a batter(or at least a bat-swinging machine) of a specified size and/or weight, which should include a baseball bat.

2. The model will have to have a function where they are activated, and they hit a ball either as far as possible or as often as possible.

3. The batter will have to hit a ball about the size of an gum ball.

4. You will get 3 to 10 attempts to make a hit. If your player device falls down, misses the ball, or breaks during an attempt, it is considered a failure.

5. The best scoring team may be calculated either by hitting average or by longest hits (home runs).

MATERIALS:

INSTRUCTOR MATERIALS:

• Model baseball diamond or flat surface (a smooth table, a floor, or sheet of melamine to make your diamond on). Decorate your diamond with at least home plate and a pitcher's mound.

• Scale models of baseball

• Accurate pitching or throwing device

PARTICIPANT MATERIALS:

• paper clips

• rubber bands

• scissors

• dowel rods and popsicle sticks

• tape and glue

• foam

• brass fasteners

• string

• other approved materials

GRADED ASSIGNMENT SUGGESTIONS:

Grading suggestions include:

• a write-up of ideas, including blueprints

• grade results based upon the execution of the model and how accurately it reflects the proposed ideas

• a project about a specific batter or a fielder's position in baseball

• an infographic about batting stats in baseball

STANDARDS: DISTANCE, ENERGY, FORCES, MEASUREMENT, MOTION

BASEBALL: HOME TEAM JERSEYS

Jerseys are a big part of any team in any sport. They're part psychology, part marketing, and part inspiration for a team. Design your own jersey for a team, either fictional or real!

MISSION RULES AND RESTRICTIONS:

1. Research baseball jerseys and uniforms.
2. Use your research to help you design the perfect baseball uniform. Optionally, make alternate color schemes for away games or alternate home jerseys.
3. Create a model of your jersey idea.
4. Also create an advertising scheme or sales pitch to present to your peers. Your presentation might include a pitch for a city that does not currently have a team.
5. Optionally, design a field layout that reflects the team logo and theme.

MATERIALS:

INSTRUCTOR MATERIALS:

- student access to internet for research
- jersey examples
- optionally, miniature models or mannikins to place jerseys on.

PARTICIPANT MATERIALS:

- fabric, including athletic fabrics
- tape and glue
- colored tape
- paint
- sewing and design materials
- scissors
- other approved, scavenged materials
- access to printing for designs and logos

GRADED ASSIGNMENT SUGGESTIONS:

Grading suggestions include:

- a write-up of ideas, including blueprints
- grade results based upon the execution of the model and how accurately it reflects the proposed ideas
- a project about logos, team mascots, or a particular sports arena where baseball is played
- the history of a team name, especially one that has changed and moved around

STANDARDS: DESIGN, MATERIALS, MODELS

BASEBALL: NO HITTER

The mental game in baseball is usually between the batter and the pitcher. What pitch to throw, where to aim, how fast to throw it, where are you in the count... So many things to think about! Design a strikeout machine!

MISSION RULES AND RESTRICTIONS:

1. Create a baseball player model of a pitcher (or at least a bat-swinging machine) of a specified size and/or weight, which should include a baseball bat.

2. The model will have to have a function where they are activated, and they throw a ball at a strike zone.

3. The pitcher will have to accurately throw a ball about the size of an gum ball.

4. You will get several attempts to throw the ball and strike out batters. If your player device falls down, drops the ball, misses the strike zone, hits a batter, or breaks during an attempt, it is considered a failure (or ball).

5. The best scoring team will be calculated by accuracy, according to a balls and strikes count.

GRADED ASSIGNMENT SUGGESTIONS:

Grading suggestions include:

- a write-up of ideas, including blueprints

- grade results based upon the execution of the model and how accurately it reflects the proposed ideas

- a project about a specific pitcher in baseball

- an infographic about pitching stats in baseball

MATERIALS:

INSTRUCTOR MATERIALS:

- Model baseball diamond or flat surface (a smooth table, a floor, or sheet of melamine to make your diamond on). Decorate your diamond with at least home plate and a pitcher's mound.

- Scale models of baseball

- Optionally, batter and catcher models

PARTICIPANT MATERIALS:

- paper clips

- rubber bands

- scissors

- card stock

- popsicle sticks

- tape and glue

- foam

- brass fasteners

- string

- other approved materials

STANDARDS: ACCURACY, ENERGY, FORCES, MOTION, STATISTICS

BASEBALL: STEALING FIRST

Stealing bases is one of the best ways to advance a runner. Done right, it's a great way to give your team an advantage. Design a base runner that can slide into a base.

MISSION RULES AND RESTRICTIONS:

1. Create a baseball player model of a specified size and/or weight, which should include recognizable baseball gear.

2. The model will have to have a function where they are activated, and they slide into a base or home plate.

3. There may or may not be a baseman or catcher waiting to tag you out. If so, you will have to slide under their tag.

4. You will get 3 to 5 attempts to slide into the base. If your player falls down, doesn't reach the base, or slides past the base, it is considered an out.

MATERIALS:

INSTRUCTOR MATERIALS:

• Model baseball diamond or flat surface (a smooth table, a floor, or sheet of melamine to make your diamond on). Decorate your diamond with at least two bases and/or a home plate

• Optionally, basemen and catcher models

PARTICIPANT MATERIALS:

• paper clips

• rubber bands

• card stock

• scissors

• popsicle sticks

• tape and glue

• foam

• brass fasteners

• string

• other approved materials

GRADED ASSIGNMENT SUGGESTIONS:

Grading suggestions include:

• a write-up of ideas, including blueprints

• grade results based upon if the device actually works, and, if so, how successfully?

• a reflection based on the experiences

• a report on the history of stealing bases in baseball

• a report on a famous base stealer in baseball

STANDARDS: ACCURACY, FORCES, FRICTION, MOTION, NEWTON'S LAWS

BASKETBALL

BASKETBALL-THEMED SPORTS PROJECTS

INSTRUCTOR NOTES:

SOME OF THESE PROJECTS REQUIRE YOU TO BUILD PARTS OF A MODEL BASKETBALL COURT. BUILDING THEM MAY BE TIME AND MATERIAL INTENSIVE. PLAN AHEAD AND SHOP AROUND FOR MATERIALS AND PIECES THAT MAKE THE PROJECT EASIER AND MORE AFFORDABLE.

BASKETBALL: BOUNCE PASS

Passing is a key way to get the ball from one player to another to move it down the court. Bounce passes are a great way to get the ball past defenders when chest passes or lobs down the court might be intercepted. Build a device to bounce a ball and one to catch it.

MISSION RULES AND RESTRICTIONS:

1. Watch a video of a bounce pass and/or other passing techniques.

2. Design a device that will, when activated, toss and bounce a ball toward a second device, the receiving device. The second device will be set a specified distance from the first device, such as 6 or 12 inches.

3. The receiving device doesn't have to move, but it should accurately 'catch' the ball on its own or when activated.

4. The receiving spot of the second device may not be more than twice the diameter of the ball.

5. Repetition is key. Your devices must be able to accurately repeat the motion without dropping or missing the ball.

6. A set number of trials, such as 5 or 10 will be done. Try to make your project as accurate as possible.

GRADED ASSIGNMENT SUGGESTIONS:

Grading suggestions include:

• a write-up of ideas, including blueprints

• grade results based upon if the device actually works, and, if so, how successfully?

• a report on passing in the sport of basketball

• an actual passing exercise/trick done in person with a teammate

MATERIALS:

INSTRUCTOR MATERIALS:

• Model basketball court or flat surface

• Orange scale models of basketballs or bouncy balls

• Rulers

PARTICIPANT MATERIALS:

• Plastic spoons

• Serving cups

• Tape and glue

• Paper clips

• Springs

• Rubber bands

• Popsicle sticks

• Notecards

• Plastic straws

• Other scavenged building materials

STANDARDS: ACCURACY, FORCE, GRAVITY, MOTION, TASK COMPLETION, TRAJECTORIES

BASKETBALL: BRACKETS

Basketball tournaments usually require brackets of 8, 16, 32, or even 64 teams. They're a visual representation of which teams play each other and which team(s) continue on toward the final championship round. Devise an infographic or alternative solution for brackets.

MISSION RULES AND RESTRICTIONS:

1. Research brackets and other methods of organizing tournament match-ups and results.
2. Create a graphic organizer, infographic, computer site, or 3D model of a different type to display the same information in a new way.
3. Share your method.

MATERIALS:

INSTRUCTOR MATERIALS:

• Example of a tournament bracket

• Access to computers

PARTICIPANT MATERIALS:

Materials will vary heavily, but may include:

• Paper

• Markers

• Labeling and design materials

• Computers

• Printers

• Internet Access

GRADED ASSIGNMENT SUGGESTIONS:

Grading suggestions include:

• a write-up of ideas, including blueprints

• grade results based upon the practicality of the design for recording tournament match-ups and results

• a report on a basketball tournament

STANDARDS: DATA, DESIGN, ORGANIZATION, TECHNOLOGY

BASKETBALL: FAST BREAK

A 'fast break' is when offensive players make a quick series of moves and passes to get past the defenders, creating scoring opportunities. Make a series of devices that can pass a ball forward from one to the next as fast as possible.

MISSION RULES AND RESTRICTIONS:

1. Watch a video of a fast break in basketball.

2. Design a set of device that will, when activated, toss and bounce a ball toward a second relay device, which will relay it to a final shooting device, which will shoot it at a hoop.

3. The relay device will have a receiver. The receiving spot of the second device may not be more than twice the diameter of the ball. This device will be activated to pass to the final shooting device.

4. When activated, the final shooting device should shoot the ball at a hoop, which will be placed nearby.

5. Repetition is key. Your devices must be able to accurately repeat the motions without dropping balls or missing shots.

6. A set number of trials, such as 5 or 10 will be done. Try to make your project as accurate as possible.

MATERIALS:

INSTRUCTOR MATERIALS:

- Model basketball court with at least 1 hoop, backboard, and lines

- Orange scale models of basketballs or bouncy balls

PARTICIPANT MATERIALS:

- Plastic spoons

- Serving cups

- Tape and glue

- Paper clips

- Springs

- Rubber bands

- Popsicle sticks

- Notecards

- Plastic straws

- Other scavenged building materials

GRADED ASSIGNMENT SUGGESTIONS:

Grading suggestions include:

- a write-up of ideas, including blueprints

- grade results based upon if the device actually works, and, if so, how successfully?

- a report on offensive and defensive stats in basketball

- a presentation on fast breaks, such as a highlight real, an interactive website, or other multimedia project

STANDARDS: ACCURACY, FORCE, GRAVITY, MOTION, TRAJECTORIES

BASKETBALL: HOME COURT ADVANTAGE

Basketball is played on a wooden court with a number of lines that help determine scoring and other rules. Design your own custom court with optional 'house rules.'

MISSION RULES AND RESTRICTIONS:

1. Research the design of a basketball court, paying special attention to the lines and zones of the court. Include research on how the game is played around those areas, such as the half-court line, the 3-point line, etc...

2. Redesign basketball play, adding several new rules and modifications to the classic design of the lines and zones of the court. Position of lines, changes of dimensions, or added areas are some possible alterations.

3. Present your idea (with a model if possible).

4. If possible, play a game on a modified court. This may be reserved for the game modification chosen as the best of the group.

GRADED ASSIGNMENT SUGGESTIONS:

Grading suggestions include:

• a write-up of ideas, including blueprints

• grade results based upon if the device actually works, and, if so, how successfully?

• a report on a basketball arena, the court surfaces and construction, or on the history of basketball court lines and rules

MATERIALS:

INSTRUCTOR MATERIALS:

• Actual basketball court if possible, or pictures of a real court

PARTICIPANT MATERIALS:

• Poster board or thin wooden sheets

• Access to printers

• Colored tapes

• Markers

• Netting

• Paint

• Plastic straws

• Paper clips

• Foam sheeting

STANDARDS: DESIGN, MEASUREMENT, MODELS

BASKETBALL: HOOP DRILLS

Basketball is all about getting that orange ball into the hoop. Create a device that can accurately shoot basketballs on a scale-sized court.

MISSION RULES AND RESTRICTIONS:

1. You will design a ball-shooting device, which may or may not look like a player. The device should have a spot to put the ball on, which can then be fired and reloaded.

2. You will get a set amount of time, such as 30 seconds, to sink as many free throws, 2, or 3 pointers as possible.

3. Practice and design for accuracy, easy repetition, and potentially for adjustability (so it can shoot from different spots).

4. Multiple rounds of scoring may occur, depending on available time.

5. You may only use approved materials and the approved amounts of materials. Your projects must also fit within approved dimensions.

6. Limited testing opportunities may be available prior to actual trials.

GRADED ASSIGNMENT SUGGESTIONS:

Grading suggestions include:

- a write-up of ideas, including blueprints

- grade results based upon if the device actually works, and, if so, how successfully?

- a report on types of shots in basketball, as well as critical statistics about those shots

- a mock-up of a basketball card for a player of your choice

MATERIALS:

INSTRUCTOR MATERIALS:

- Model basketball court with at least 1 hoop, backboard, and lines

- Orange scale models of basketballs

- Scoreboard and timer

PARTICIPANT MATERIALS:

- Plastic spoons and straws

- Tape and glue

- Paper clips

- Springs

- Rubber bands

- Popsicle sticks

- Other scavenged building materials

STANDARDS: ACCURACY, FORCE, GRAVITY, MOTION, TRAJECTORIES

BASKETBALL: HOOP IT UP

Basketball was originally played with baskets hanging on a wall, and the ball had to be removed after every basket. Things have come a long way! Design your own hoop from scratch. Pay special attention to key features of the post, the backboard, the rim, and the net.

MISSION RULES AND RESTRICTIONS:

1. Research the dimensions and styles of modern and historical basketball hoops and backboards.
2. Design an accurate scale model of one of these hoop/backboards, or create a modified new version.
3. Create a model of your ideas.
4. Share your model, along with explanations of how it changed or would change the game.

TEACHERS OPTION: Optionally, create a series of models to show changes over time (each era's design could be assigned to a different team).

GRADED ASSIGNMENT SUGGESTIONS:

Grading suggestions include:

- a write-up of ideas, including blueprints

- grade results based upon how accurate and realistic the hoop is

- a report on materials and measurements of hoops/backboards

MATERIALS:

INSTRUCTOR MATERIALS:

- Rulers

- Possibly pictures of modern and historical backboards/hoops

PARTICIPANT MATERIALS:

- Plastic straws

- Tape and glue

- Paper clips

- Mesh or netting

- Rubber bands

- Popsicle sticks

- PVS tubing

- Clear plastic sheeting

- Foam

- Colored tapes

- Paint

- Other scavenged building materials

STANDARDS: DESIGN, ENGINEERING, MEASUREMENT, MODELS

BASKETBALL: JERSEY CITY

Create a jersey for a fictional or real basketball team.

MISSION RULES AND RESTRICTIONS:

1. Research basketball jerseys.
2. Use your research to help you design the perfect basketball jersey. Optionally, make alternate color schemes for away games or alternate home jerseys.
3. Create a model of your jersey idea.
4. Also create an advertising scheme or sales pitch to present to your peers. Your presentation might include a pitch for a city that does not currently have a team.
5. Optionally, design an arena layout that reflects the team logo and theme.

MATERIALS:

INSTRUCTOR MATERIALS:

- Student access to internet for research
- Jersey examples
- Optionally, miniature models or mannikins to place jerseys on.

PARTICIPANT MATERIALS:

- Fabric, including athletic fabrics
- Tape and glue
- Colored tape
- Paint
- Sewing and design materials
- Scissors
- Other approved, scavenged materials
- Access to printing for designs and logo

GRADED ASSIGNMENT SUGGESTIONS:

Grading suggestions include:

- a write-up of ideas, including blueprints
- grade results based upon the execution of the model and how accurately it reflects the proposed ideas
- a project about logos, team mascots, or a particular sports arena where basketball is played

STANDARDS: DESIGN, MATERIALS, MODELS

BASKETBALL: NEW KICKS

Basketball has little in the way of equipment other than the uniform and shoes. Shoes are probably the key piece of equipment in the sport, besides the ball, of course. Design a pair of high-tech shoes that might give you an advantage in the game!

MISSION RULES AND RESTRICTIONS:

1. Research athletic footwear and animals with great jumping abilities.
2. Use your research to help you design the perfect basketball shoe.
3. Create a model of your shoe idea.
4. Also create an advertising scheme or sales pitch to present to your peers.

MATERIALS:

INSTRUCTOR MATERIALS:

• Student access to internet for research

PARTICIPANT MATERIALS:

• Fabric, including heavier fabrics and rubber-type materials

• Tape and glue

• Rubber bands

• Colored tape

• Paint

• Clay

• Eyelets and shoelaces

• Sewing and design materials

• Scissors

• Other approved, scavenged materials

GRADED ASSIGNMENT SUGGESTIONS:

Grading suggestions include:

• a write-up of ideas, including blueprints

• grade results based upon the execution of the model and how accurately it reflects the proposed ideas

• a report on shoes, footwear, or a shoe brand

• a project about feet and/or leg muscles

STANDARDS: ANATOMY, DESIGN, ERGONOMICS, MATERIALS, MODELS

BASKETBALL: ROBOTS CAN JUMP

One key skill in basketball is jumping. If you're defending, passing, or trying to score, you're probably running and jumping. Build a model player that can jump as high as possible.

MISSION RULES AND RESTRICTIONS:

1. You will design a jumping model of a player. It will jump when activated.

2. Your project should resemble a player, even if it is just a picture of a player attached to the outside of the mechanism.

3. Your device must fit within dimensions specified by your instructor, possibly to fit a model basketball court.

4. You will have multiple attempts to jump your project. Either and average, the highest jump, or both will be considered for the 'best' project.

MATERIALS:

INSTRUCTOR MATERIALS:

• Model basketball court with at least 1 hoop, backboard, and lines

• Orange scale models of basketballs

• Pictures of basketball players

• Rulers

PARTICIPANT MATERIALS:

• Tape and glue

• Paper clips

• Springs

• Rubber bands

• Popsicle sticks

• PVC pipes (small gauge)

• Other scavenged building materials

GRADED ASSIGNMENT SUGGESTIONS:

Grading suggestions include:

• a write-up of ideas, including blueprints

• grade results based upon if the device actually works, and, if so, how successfully?

• a report on a particularly good jumper (in basketball or nature) and any information you can find on the mechanics of jumping

• a collage or media presentation about jumping and/or slam dunks and alley oops.

STANDARDS: DEVICES, FORCE, GRAVITY, HEIGHT, MOTION

BASKETBALL: SHOT BLOCKERS

You can't score if you can't get the ball to the hoop! Build a device that can block shots from a hoop shooting model player.

MISSION RULES AND RESTRICTIONS:

1. Your instructor will have a shooting device that will attempt to make shots in a model hoop.

2. You will have to block as many shots as possible in a set amount of time and/or limit the points that can be scored during the set time.

3. Your device may jump, swat at the ball, or otherwise attempt to block the shots. However, your blocking device may not slap or make contact with the shooting device. Nor may it cover the hoop and goaltend.

4. The devices may be adjusted and moved between shots, but adjustment time may be limited to a few seconds.

5. Your device must fit within certain dimensions, depending on the scale of the basketball court and hoop.

MATERIALS:

INSTRUCTOR MATERIALS:

- Model basketball court with at least 1 hoop, backboard, and lines

- A ball-shooting device (adjustable if possible)

- Orange scale models of basketballs

PARTICIPANT MATERIALS:

- Plastic spoons and straws

- Tape and glue

- Serving cups

- Paper clips

- Springs

- Rubber bands

- Notecards

- Popsicle sticks

- Other scavenged building materials

GRADED ASSIGNMENT SUGGESTIONS:

Grading suggestions include:

- a write-up of ideas, including blueprints

- grade results based upon if the device actually works, and, if so, how successfully?

- a report on defensive stats like rebounds and blocks in basketball

- a mock-up of a basketball card for a great defensive player in basketball

STANDARDS: ACCURACY, FORCE, MOTION, TRAJECTORIES

FOOTBALL

FOOTBALL-THEMED SPORTS PROJECTS

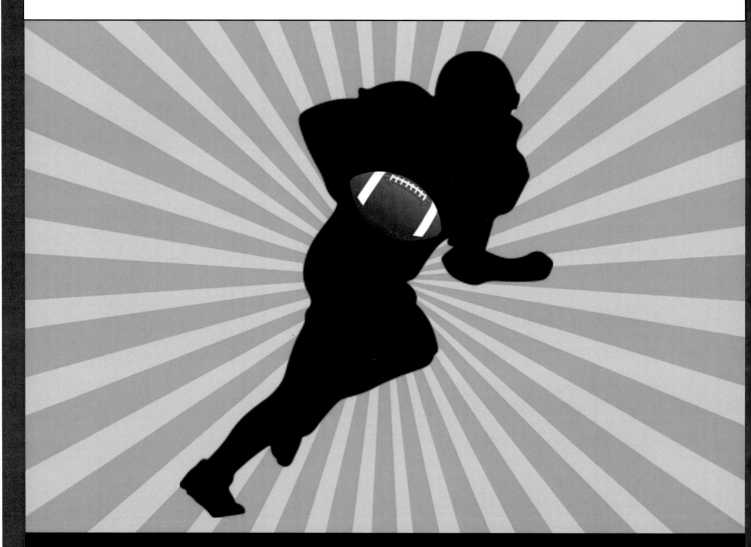

INSTRUCTOR NOTES:

SOME OF THESE PROJECTS REQUIRE YOU TO BUILD PARTS OF A MODEL FOOTBALL FIELD. BUILDING THEM MAY BE TIME AND MATERIAL INTENSIVE. PLAN AHEAD AND SHOP AROUND FOR MATERIALS AND PIECES THAT MAKE THE PROJECT EASIER AND MORE AFFORDABLE.

FOOTBALL: FAIR CATCH

Games and each offensive series start with a kick and a catch, followed by crashing players. Create a punt returner model that can catch a falling or punted ball.

MISSION RULES AND RESTRICTIONS:

1. Design a device or model that can catch a falling ball.

2. The ball will be dropped in a consistent manner from a specified height and/or at a specified angle.

3. Your device must be designed from provided and/or approved materials only.

4. Test and redesign to have the best punt returner. Testing opportunities may be limited.

5. Final scoring might depend either on accuracy (best out of 5 or 10 attempts). If the ball pops out of the receiver's hands or drops, it counts as a fail. Misses may be do-overs.

6. Additional tests might be done at varying heights or angles to asses the versatility of your catching system.

GRADED ASSIGNMENT SUGGESTIONS:

Grading suggestions include:

- a write-up of ideas, including blueprints

- grade results based upon if the device actually works, and, if so, how successfully?

- a report on punt and kick returns in the sport of football

- a mock-up of a football card for a kick returner or other special teams position

MATERIALS:

INSTRUCTOR MATERIALS:

- possibly a delivery system for the footballs to create a consistent drop, such as a tube anchored in place to drop them through

- mini footballs

PARTICIPANT MATERIALS:

- notecards or card stock

- markers and crayons

- tape and glue

- paperclips

- clothespins

- rubber bands

- popsicle sticks

- fabric

- toothpicks

- clay or playdough

STANDARDS: ACCURACY, GRAVITY

FOOTBALL: FIELD GOAL KICKERS

Sometimes, games are decided by kickers. They put in those extra points. They blast those long kicks for 3 point field goals when touchdowns are unattainable. Create a device that can accurately kick field goals at varying distances.

MISSION RULES AND RESTRICTIONS:

1. Design a device that can be operated to kick, flick, or hit a ball through a pair of uprights.

2. The field goal posts will be provided by your teacher, and may be constructed from pipe, straws, or other materials, depending on scale.

3. Your device must be designed from provided and/or approved materials only.

4. Test and redesign to have the best kicker. Testing opportunities may be limited.

5. Final scoring might depend either on accuracy (best out of 5 or 10 attempts) or on distance.

GRADED ASSIGNMENT SUGGESTIONS:

Grading suggestions include:

• a write-up of ideas, including blueprints

• grade results based upon if the device actually works, and, if so, how successfully?

• a report on placekicking in the sport of football

• a mock-up of a football card for a kicker or punter

MATERIALS:

INSTRUCTOR MATERIALS:

• goalposts to test with

• mini field with marked off distances

• mini footballs (play-dough, rubber, erasers, or otherwise)

• measuring tape

PARTICIPANT MATERIALS:

• notecards or card stock

• markers and crayons

• tape and glue

• paperclips

• string

• clothespins

• rubber bands

• popsicle sticks

• small springs

• thread spools

STANDARDS: ACCURACY, DISTANCE, FORCE, MACHINES

FOOTBALL: HAIL MARY

In the last seconds of a half or a game, sometimes the quarterback just goes deep, praying for that catch that can change the game. Create a quarterback model that can throw some deep passes.

MISSION RULES AND RESTRICTIONS:

1. Design a device or player model that can be operated to throw a ball as far as possible.

2. Mini footballs will be provided by your teacher.

3. A drop or 'misfire' of your device may be counted as an incomplete throw or may be measured from the drop point.

4. Your device must be designed from provided and/or approved materials only.

5. Test and redesign to have the best quarterback. Testing opportunities may be limited.

6. Final scoring might depend either on average pass length or longest pass distance.

GRADED ASSIGNMENT SUGGESTIONS:

Grading suggestions include:

• a write-up of ideas, including blueprints

• grade results based upon if the device actually works, and, if so, how successfully?

• a report on passing records and/or Hail Mary's in the sport of football

• a mock-up of a football card for a quarterback

MATERIALS:

INSTRUCTOR MATERIALS:

• mini field with marked off distances (or floorspace and a measuring tape)

• mini footballs

PARTICIPANT MATERIALS:

• notecards or card stock

• markers and crayons

• tape and glue

• paperclips

• string

• clothespins

• rubber bands

• popsicle sticks

• small springs

• thread spools

STANDARDS: DISTANCE, FLIGHT, FORCE, KINETIC ENERGY, LEVERS, MACHINES

FOOTBALL: MODEL PLAYER

Create a model of the protective gear a player may need to play in football. Consider safety risks and potential injuries when designing.

MISSION RULES AND RESTRICTIONS:

1. Create a model of a player in their gear. The more detail the better. Realism is a plus!

2. Draw inspiration from current and historical uniforms and gear, other sports, and other careers where personal protection is necessary.

3. Your model must be designed from provided and/or approved materials only.

4. Judges will score your designs for practicality, looks, and innovation.

TEACHER'S OPTION: have each team design just a piece of the uniform, such as a pad, helmet, jersey, cleat, gloves, etc...

GRADED ASSIGNMENT SUGGESTIONS:

Grading suggestions include:

• a write-up of ideas, including blueprints

• grades based on judging assessments of designs

• a sales pitch or advertisement for your designs

MATERIALS:

INSTRUCTOR MATERIALS:

• judging cards based on specific criteria, like practicality, looks, and innovation

PARTICIPANT MATERIALS:

• notecards or card stock

• markers and crayons

• tape and glue

• paperclips

• string and thread

• clothespins

• rubber bands

• popsicle sticks

• fabric

• scissors

• velcro

• foam

• clay

STANDARDS: DESIGN, ENGINEERING, USING TOOLS

FOOTBALL: PASS RUSH

If a quarterback has all day to make plays happen, it can be really hard to win. Create a model of a defensive player that can break through an offensive line and get a sack.

MISSION RULES AND RESTRICTIONS:

1. Design a moving device that can be operated to push through a line of model defenders to reach a quarterback.

2. When triggered, your device should push through a model wall of the offensive line to reach the model quarterback.

3. A specific scale of players will be determined. Yours should be close in parameters.

4. Your device must be designed from provided and/or approved materials only.

5. Test and redesign to have the best pass rusher. Testing opportunities may be limited.

6. Final scoring might depend either on accuracy (best out of 5 or 10 attempts). Reaching and coming in contact with the quarterback is considered success.

GRADED ASSIGNMENT SUGGESTIONS:

Grading suggestions include:

• a write-up of ideas, including blueprints

• grade results based upon if the device actually works, and, if so, how successfully?

• a report on quarterback sacks in the sport of football

• a mock-up of a football card for a defensive player

MATERIALS:

INSTRUCTOR MATERIALS:

• models of an offensive line and a quarterback, even something as simple as pictures glued onto plastic cups

• model of field, or a table/ flat area to test on

PARTICIPANT MATERIALS:

• notecards or card stock

• markers and crayons

• tape and glue

• paperclips

• string

• clothespins

• rubber bands

• popsicle sticks

• small springs

• thread spools

STANDARDS: FORCE, MACHINES, MOTION

FOOTBALL: PIGSKINS

Footballs are supposed to be a very specific size, shape, and weight, and must even be inflated to the correct pressure. Create a football from scratch! What features make your ball better than existing ones?

MISSION RULES AND RESTRICTIONS:

1. Design a football from scratch.

2. Your device must be designed from provided and/or approved materials only.

3. Your teacher will give you specific min/max weight, length, and circumference guidelines you must meet to make a qualifying football.

4. Test throwing the ball. Design and redesign for the best throwing ball possible.

5. Test and redesign to have the best ball. Testing opportunities may be limited.

6. Final scoring might depend either on distance, ease of throwing and catching, or its ability to fly in a spiral.

GRADED ASSIGNMENT SUGGESTIONS:

Grading suggestions include:

- a write-up of ideas, including blueprints

- grade results based upon if the device actually works, and, if so, how successfully?

- a report on footballs, how they are made, and what they are made from

- a sales ad for your own unique brand/style of football

MATERIALS:

INSTRUCTOR MATERIALS:

- measuring tape

- open area to throw balls around

PARTICIPANT MATERIALS:

Materials will vary according to what teachers provide and what can be scavenged, but may include:

- foam

- plastic

- cardboard

- bubble wrap

- plastic wrap

- cotton balls

- tape

- balloons

- textured fabrics

- etc...

STANDARDS: ACCURACY, DESIGN, DISTANCE, FLIGHT

FOOTBALL: TACKLED!

If a running back finds open holes and can find some open ground, he can be hard to stop. Create a model of a defensive player that can intercept a running player and knock them down.

MISSION RULES AND RESTRICTIONS:

1. Design a moving device that can be operated to run over to a moving opposing player and knock them down. When triggered, your device should run toward, catch, and knock down a model running back.

2. A specific scale of players will be determined. Yours should be close in parameters.

3. Your device must be designed from provided and/or approved materials only.

4. Test and redesign to have the best pass rusher. Testing opportunities may be limited.

5. Final scoring might depend either on accuracy (best out of 5 or 10 attempts). Coming in contact with the running back vs. actually knocking down the running back might be scored differently.

MATERIALS:

INSTRUCTOR MATERIALS:

• a moving model of a running back.

• models of an offensive line and a quarterback, even something as simple as pictures glued onto plastic cups

• model of field, or a table/ flat area to test on

PARTICIPANT MATERIALS:

• notecards or card stock

• markers and crayons

• tape and glue

• paperclips

• string

• clothespins

• rubber bands

• popsicle sticks

• small springs

• thread spools

GRADED ASSIGNMENT SUGGESTIONS:

Grading suggestions include:

• a write-up of ideas, including blueprints

• grade results based upon if the device actually works, and, if so, how successfully?

• a report on tackling techniques, highlights, etc...

• a mock-up of a football card for a defensive player

STANDARDS: ACCURACY, FORCE, MACHINES, MOTION

FOOTBALL: TOUCHDOWN!

Passing is pretty exciting, but watching a running back break tackles and put one in the end zone can be really fun to watch! Create a model of a running back that can break through a defensive line and score a touchdown.

MISSION RULES AND RESTRICTIONS:

1. Design a moving device that can be operated to push through a line of model defenders to reach an end zone.

2. When triggered, your device should push through a model defense to reach an end zone. The defensive players may or may not move, and may or may not attempt to tackle.

3. A specific scale of players will be determined. Yours should be close in parameters.

4. Your device must be designed from provided and/or approved materials only.

5. Test and redesign to have the best running back. Testing opportunities may be limited.

6. Final scoring might depend either on accuracy (best out of 5 or 10 attempts). You must cross into the end zone to succeed.

MATERIALS:

INSTRUCTOR MATERIALS:

- models of a defensive line and secondary defensive players. Even something as simple as pictures glued onto plastic cups

- model of field, or a table/ flat area to test on

PARTICIPANT MATERIALS:

- notecards or card stock

- markers and crayons

- tape and glue

- paperclips

- string

- clothespins

- rubber bands

- popsicle sticks

- small springs

- thread spools

GRADED ASSIGNMENT SUGGESTIONS:

Grading suggestions include:

- a write-up of ideas, including blueprints

- grade results based upon if the device actually works, and, if so, how successfully?

- a report or infographic on running vs passing in the NFL

- a mock-up of a football card for a running back

STANDARDS: DISTANCE, FORCE, MACHINES, MOTION

FOOTBALL: VIBRATING FOOTBALL

Create a vibrating model of a football field along with scale models of players for two teams. Let the field vibrate to see how plays turn out!

MISSION RULES AND RESTRICTIONS:

1. Design a vibrating or shaking football field.

2. Major details of the field, such as field goal posts, end zones, paint lines, and other pieces should be identifiable.

3. Create two teams of standing players that fit the scale of your field.

4. Your field should vibrate and players should move when operated. Test and redesign to make sure players actually move.

5. Your device must be designed from provided and/or approved materials only.

6. Final scoring might depend on overall detail of the project and the players

7. Optionally, operate players through the bottom of the field with magnets.

GRADED ASSIGNMENT SUGGESTIONS:

Grading suggestions include:

- a write-up of ideas, including blueprints

- grade results based upon if the device actually works, and, if so, how successfully?

- a report or infographic on football field statistics and measurements in the NFL and/or other sports or leagues

MATERIALS:

INSTRUCTOR MATERIALS:

- pictures of actual football fields to help with designs

PARTICIPANT MATERIALS:

- notecards or card stock

- markers and crayons

- tape and glue

- paperclips

- string

- clothespins

- rubber bands

- popsicle sticks

- small springs

- thread spools

- thin plywood or cardboard

- plastic straws

- small vibrating motors (pager motors or larger)

- magnets

STANDARDS: MACHINES, MOTION, VIBRATION

FOOTBALL: WIDE RECEIVER

Running those deep routes can be fun to watch. Create a wide receiver model that can catch a pass, even if he is being defended!

MISSION RULES AND RESTRICTIONS:

1. Design a device or model that can catch an incoming pass.

2. The ball will be launched in a consistent manner at a specified angle and speed.

3. Your device must be designed from provided and/or approved materials only.

4. Test and redesign to have the best receiver. Testing opportunities may be limited.

5. Final scoring might depend either on accuracy (best out of 5 or 10 attempts). If the ball pops out of the receiver's hands or drops, it counts as a fail. Misses may be do-overs.

6. Additional tests might be done at varying heights or angles to asses the versatility of your catching system.

MATERIALS:

INSTRUCTOR MATERIALS:

• model of field, or a table/ flat area to test on

• a delivery system for the footballs to create a consistent pass, such as a tube anchored in place to blow them through like darts

• mini footballs

PARTICIPANT MATERIALS:

• notecards or card stock

• markers and crayons

• tape and glue

• paperclips

• clothespins

• rubber bands

• popsicle sticks

• fabric

• toothpicks

• clay or playdough

GRADED ASSIGNMENT SUGGESTIONS:

Grading suggestions include:

• a write-up of ideas, including blueprints

• grade results based upon if the device actually works, and, if so, how successfully?

• a report on pass receiving in the sport of football, especially applicable statistics for those players

• a mock-up of a football card for a wide receiver

STANDARDS: ACCURACY, MACHINES, NEWTON'S LAWS

ICE HOCKEY

ICE HOCKEY-THEMED SPORTS PROJECTS

INSTRUCTOR NOTES:

SOME OF THESE PROJECTS REQUIRE YOU TO BUILD PARTS OF A MODEL HOCKEY RINK. BUILDING THEM MAY BE TIME AND MATERIAL INTENSIVE. PLAN AHEAD AND SHOP AROUND FOR MATERIALS AND PIECES THAT MAKE THE PROJECT EASIER AND MORE AFFORDABLE.

ICE HOCKEY: BLADES OF STEEL

You can't play on ice without skates, and yet ice hockey skates are different from other skates, such as figure skates or speed skating skates. Design a new and unique pair of ice skates!

MISSION RULES AND RESTRICTIONS:

1. Research ice hockey skates, as well as other kinds of ice skates.
2. Use your research to help you design the perfect ice hockey skate.
3. Create a model of your skate idea.
4. Also create an advertising scheme or sales pitch to present to your peers.

GRADED ASSIGNMENT SUGGESTIONS:

Grading suggestions include:

- a write-up of ideas, including blueprints

- grade results based upon the execution of the model and how accurately it reflects the proposed ideas

- a report on skates or a skate brand

- a project about feet and/or leg muscles

MATERIALS:

INSTRUCTOR MATERIALS:

- student access to internet for research

- actual hockey skates for comparison

PARTICIPANT MATERIALS:

- fabric, including heavier fabrics and rubber-type materials

- metal bands

- tape and glue

- rubber bands

- colored tape

- paint

- clay

- eyelets and shoelaces

- sewing and design materials

- scissors

- other approved, scavenged materials

STANDARDS: ANATOMY, DESIGN, ERGONOMICS, MATERIALS, MODELS

ICE HOCKEY: BODY CHECK

Hockey is a contact sport. If you're holding the puck and not watching around you, prepare to get leveled. Make a model player that can knock over an opponent with the puck!

MISSION RULES AND RESTRICTIONS:

1. Create a hockey player model of a specified size and/or weight, which should include a hockey stick.

2. The model will have to have a function where they are activated, and they will charge at a target, hopefully knocking them down.

3. The hockey player will have to hit a player model of a scaled size similar to yours.

4. You will get 3 to 5 attempts to make a hit. If your player falls down, misses the other player, or breaks during an attempt, it is considered a failure.

5. The best scoring team may be calculated either by knockback distance or number of successful hits/knockdowns.

GRADED ASSIGNMENT SUGGESTIONS:

Grading suggestions include:

- a write-up of ideas, including blueprints

- grade results based upon the execution of the model and how accurately it reflects the proposed ideas

- a project or infographic about penalties in hockey

MATERIALS:

INSTRUCTOR MATERIALS:

- Model hockey rink or flat surface (a smooth table, a floor, or sheet of melamine to make your rink on) decorate your rink and build a goal

- Scale models of players

PARTICIPANT MATERIALS:

- paper clips

- notecards

- springs

- scissors

- plastic straws

- tape and glue

- popsicle sticks

- rubber bands

- thread spools

- other approved materials

STANDARDS: ENERGY, FORCES, MOTION, NEWTON'S LAWS

ICE HOCKEY: FRESH JERSEYS

Jerseys are a big part of any team in any sport. They're part psychology, part marketing, and part inspiration for a team. Design your own jersey for a team, either fictional or real!

MISSION RULES AND RESTRICTIONS:

1. Research hockey jerseys.
2. Use your research to help you design the perfect hockey jersey. Optionally, make alternate color schemes for away games or alternate home jerseys.
3. Create a model of your jersey idea.
4. Also create an advertising scheme or sales pitch to present to your peers. Your presentation might include a pitch for a city that does not currently have a team.
5. Optionally, design a rink layout that reflects the team logo and theme.

MATERIALS:

INSTRUCTOR MATERIALS:

- student access to internet for research
- jersey examples
- optionally, miniature models or mannikins to place jerseys on.

PARTICIPANT MATERIALS:

- fabric, including athletic fabrics
- tape and glue
- colored tape
- paint
- sewing and design materials
- scissors
- other approved, scavenged materials
- access to printing for designs and logos

GRADED ASSIGNMENT SUGGESTIONS:

Grading suggestions include:

- a write-up of ideas, including blueprints
- grade results based upon the execution of the model and how accurately it reflects the proposed ideas
- a project about logos, team mascots, or a particular sports arena where hockey is played

STANDARDS: DESIGN, MATERIALS, MODELS

ICE HOCKEY: GOALIES

Without a goalie, the score of a hockey game would probably look like a football game. They're key for pacing the game, and for defense. Make your own goalkeeper model and practice blocking shots!

MISSION RULES AND RESTRICTIONS:

1. Create a hockey player model of a specified size and/or weight, which should include a hockey stick and goalie pads, likely with a mitt and a modified stick.

2. The model will have to be controlled in front of the goal using a method of your choosing, which may include: puppetry, wind power, magnets, or another approved method.

3. The hockey player will have to stop a puck about the size of an eraser or bottle cap from going into a goal.

4. The goal will likely be built from pipe cleaners, plastic straws, and/or onion bag netting. It should be sized relative to the players.

5. You will get 3 to 10 shots to defend (multiple rounds may be required). If your goalie fails to stop the puck from going in the net, it is considered a goal.

GRADED ASSIGNMENT SUGGESTIONS:

Grading suggestions include:

- a write-up of ideas, including blueprints

- grade results based upon the execution of the model and how accurately it reflects the proposed ideas

- a project about a specific hockey goalie or the history of the goalie position and equipment

MATERIALS:

INSTRUCTOR MATERIALS:

- Model hockey rink or flat surface (a smooth table, a floor, or sheet of melamine to make your rink on) decorate your rink and build a goal

- Scale models of nets and pucks

PARTICIPANT MATERIALS:

- paper clips

- notecards

- scissors

- plastic straws

- tape and glue

- popsicle sticks

- foam

- brass fasteners

- string

- other approved materials

STANDARDS: ACCURACY, FORCES, FRICTION, MOTION, NEWTON'S LAWS

ICE HOCKEY: HIT THE ICE

Ice Hockey is one of the fastest and toughest team sports in the world. Design a skating ice hockey player and shoot a puck into a goal!

MISSION RULES AND RESTRICTIONS:

1. Create a hockey player model of a specified size and/or weight, which should include a hockey stick.

2. The model will have to be blown across the model ice rink with a small fan or by blowing air at it through a straw.

3. The hockey player will have to push a puck about the size of an eraser or bottle cap into a goal.

4. The goal will likely be built from pipe cleaners, plastic straws, and/or onion bag netting. It should be sized relative to the players.

5. You will get 3 to 5 shots at the empty net. If your player falls down, skates past the goal, or loses the puck, it is considered a miss.

MATERIALS:

INSTRUCTOR MATERIALS:

• Model hockey rink or flat surface (a smooth table, a floor, or sheet of melamine to make your rink on) decorate your rink and build a goal

• Scale models of nets and pucks

PARTICIPANT MATERIALS:

• paper clips

• notecards

• scissors

• plastic straws or small fan

• tape and glue

• popsicle sticks

• markers and crayons

• other approved materials

GRADED ASSIGNMENT SUGGESTIONS:

Grading suggestions include:

• a write-up of ideas, including blueprints

• grade results based upon if the device actually works, and, if so, how successfully?

• a reflection based on the experiences

• a report on the history of professional ice hockey

• a stat sheet to show shots on goal and goals/misses

STANDARDS: ACCURACY, FORCES, FRICTION, MOTION, NEWTON'S LAWS

ICE HOCKEY: PUCK TIME

You can't play hockey without a puck. Get busy making your own. Make sure to experiment with the coatings, weight, and composition to get the best sliding effect.

MISSION RULES AND RESTRICTIONS:

1. Create a model hockey puck.

2. Your hockey puck should be near regulation size of 1 inch tall and 3 inches across, and should be cylindrical.

3. The model will be tested sliding across a smooth surface. Create a puck that slides as easily as possible.

4. Experiment with coatings and weight to create the best sliding effect.

5. You will get 3 to 5 attempts to slide your puck across the surface. An average an/or best distance may be considered for determining the winning project.

6. There may be a set person to slide each puck in approximately the same way to increase consistency.

GRADED ASSIGNMENT SUGGESTIONS:

Grading suggestions include:

• a write-up of ideas, including blueprints

• grade results based upon if the device actually works, and, if so, how successfully?

• a report on hockey pucks

• a project advertising a modified puck with some new feature(s) to make the game different

MATERIALS:

INSTRUCTOR MATERIALS:

• a large flat surface, ice if possible, but a smooth tile floor also works (Water could also be added to make it more slick)

• tape measure

PARTICIPANT MATERIALS:

• real hockey pucks for comparison

• clay

• tape

• plastic wrap

• cooking spray

• tin foil

• tissue paper

• metal weights

• marbles

• other approved materials, especially as coverings for the puck

STANDARDS: FORCES, FRICTION, MOTION

ICE HOCKEY: RINKY DINK

Ice hockey's rink really sets the pace and style for the game. Every now and then they play with the shapes and locations of the lines on the rink. Design your own hockey rink!

MISSION RULES AND RESTRICTIONS:

1. Research the design of a hockey rink, paying special attention to the lines and zones of the rink. Include research on how the game is played around those areas, such as the blue lines, face off circles, face off spots, goal creases, etc...

2. Redesign hockey play, adding several new rules and modifications to the classic design of the lines and zones of the rink. Position of lines, changes of dimensions, or added areas are some possible alterations.

3. Present your idea (with a model if possible).

4. If possible, play a game on a modified rink (even floor hockey style). This may be reserved for the game modification chosen as the best of the group.

GRADED ASSIGNMENT SUGGESTIONS:

Grading suggestions include:

• a write-up of ideas, including blueprints

• grade results based upon if the design actually works, and, if so, how successfully?

• a report on a hockey rink, rink surfaces and construction, or on the history of hockey rink designs and rules

MATERIALS:

INSTRUCTOR MATERIALS:

• an actual hockey rink if possible, or pictures of a real rink

PARTICIPANT MATERIALS:

• poster board

• white melamine board

• access to printers

• colored tapes

• markers

• netting

• paint

• plastic straws

• foam sheeting

• cardboard

STANDARDS: DESIGN, MEASUREMENT, MODELS

ICE HOCKEY: SLAPSHOTS

One of the more powerful shots in hockey is the slapshot. Make a model player that can wind up and deliver the fastest shots possible!

MISSION RULES AND RESTRICTIONS:

1. Create a hockey player model of a specified size and/or weight, which should include a hockey stick.

2. The model will have to have a function where they are activated, and they hit a puck either as fast as possible, with as much force as possible, or as far as possible. Accuracy is a bonus, but is not necessarily the intent.

3. The hockey player will have to hit a puck about the size of an eraser or bottle cap.

4. You will get 3 to 5 attempts to make a slapshot. If your player falls down, misses the puck, or breaks during an attempt, it is considered a failure.

5. The best scoring team may be calculated either by average or by single longest/fastest shot.

GRADED ASSIGNMENT SUGGESTIONS:

Grading suggestions include:

• a write-up of ideas, including blueprints

• grade results based upon the execution of the model and how accurately it reflects the proposed ideas

• a project about a specific hockey offensive player or an offensive position, such as a center, right wing, or left wing.

MATERIALS:

INSTRUCTOR MATERIALS:

• a long, flat surface

• measuring tape

• scale models of pucks

• stopwatch (for speed calculations, if desired)

• small items to knock over (if force is measured)

PARTICIPANT MATERIALS:

• paper clips

• notecards

• scissors

• plastic straws

• tape and glue

• popsicle sticks

• rubber bands

• thread spools

• other approved materials

STANDARDS: DISTANCE, ENERGY, FORCES, MEASUREMENT, MOTION

ICE HOCKEY: STICK TO THE GAME

You can't play hockey without skates, a puck, and a stick. Design a model hockey stick of your own!

MISSION RULES AND RESTRICTIONS:

1. Research hockey sticks.
2. Use your research to help you design the perfect hockey stick.
3. Create a model of your hockey stick idea.
4. Also create an advertising scheme or sales pitch to present to your peers.
5. Optionally, test the stick if it is of a knee hockey or full-size variety.

GRADED ASSIGNMENT SUGGESTIONS:

Grading suggestions include:

- a write-up of ideas, including blueprints

- grade results based upon the execution of the model and how accurately it reflects the proposed ideas

- a project about hockey sticks, the history of hockey sticks, or infographics about the brands of hockey sticks and their prevalence

MATERIALS:

INSTRUCTOR MATERIALS:

- student access to internet for research

- hockey stick examples

- optionally, miniature models of players to put the sticks next to

PARTICIPANT MATERIALS:

- tape and glue

- colored tapes

- paint

- wood, especially balsa wood and popsicle sticks

- rigid plastic

- scissors

- access to printing for designs, logos, and letters

- other approved, scavenged materials

STANDARDS: DESIGN, MATERIALS, MODELS

ICE HOCKEY: SUIT UP

Ice hockey is a contact sport. It'd be dangerous to play without the pads. Research the pads and gear a hockey player wears, and make modifications to them to change how the sport is played!

MISSION RULES AND RESTRICTIONS:

1. Research hockey pads, helmets, and gear.
2. Use your research to help you design the perfect hockey gear.
3. Create a model of your safety equipment.
4. Also create an advertising scheme or sales pitch to present to your peers. Your presentation might include a pitch for a city that does not currently have a team.

GRADED ASSIGNMENT SUGGESTIONS:

Grading suggestions include:

- a write-up of ideas, including blueprints
- grade results based upon the practicality of the design and the effectiveness of the sales pitch
- a report on a hockey safety equipment as it has changed over time

MATERIALS:

INSTRUCTOR MATERIALS:

- student access to internet for research
- equipment samples
- Optionally, miniature models or mannikins to place equipment on.

PARTICIPANT MATERIALS:

- fabric, including athletic fabrics
- tape and glue
- colored tape
- paint
- Sewing and design materials
- Scissors
- foam sheeting
- clay
- Other approved, scavenged materials

STANDARDS: DESIGN, MATERIALS, MODELS

SOCCER

SOCCER-THEMED SPORTS PROJECTS

INSTRUCTOR NOTES:

SOME OF THESE PROJECTS REQUIRE YOU TO BUILD PARTS OF A MODEL SOCCER FIELD. BUILDING THEM MAY BE TIME AND MATERIAL INTENSIVE. PLAN AHEAD AND SHOP AROUND FOR MATERIALS AND PIECES THAT MAKE THE PROJECT EASIER AND MORE AFFORDABLE.

You can't play soccer without a ball. Get busy making your own. Make sure to experiment with the geometry in the ball's design.

MISSION RULES AND RESTRICTIONS:

1. Examine a classic soccer ball.

2. Experiment with different geometrical patterns. Figure out which shapes will best cover a ball. Try to avoid the standard pentagon/hexagon classic pattern.

3. Build a model of the design if possible. You may need to just coat or cover a standard ball with your new geometric design.

4. Your soccer ball should be near regulation size of about 8.65 inches in diameter and 27 inches in circumference, unless otherwise stated.

MATERIALS:

INSTRUCTOR MATERIALS:

• real soccer balls for comparison

• tape measure

• geometric shapes or stencils to trace

PARTICIPANT MATERIALS:

• fabric

• paper

• markers, crayons, and other coloring materials

• other approved materials, especially as coverings for the ball

GRADED ASSIGNMENT SUGGESTIONS:

Grading suggestions include:

• a write-up of ideas, including blueprints

• grade results based upon if the device actually works, and, if so, how successfully?

• a report on soccer balls

• a project advertising a modified ball with some new feature(s) to make the game different

| STANDARDS: | DESIGN, GEOMETRY, TESSELLATIONS |

SOCCER: CORNER KICKERS

One of the most strategic events in soccer is the corner kick. You get one after a defensive player touches a ball that goes out of bounds past the goal line without scoring. It looks like kicking a ball over a fence, and then anything can happen! Make a model player that can kick a penalty kick!

MISSION RULES AND RESTRICTIONS:

1. Watch videos of corner kicks.

2. Create a soccer player model of a specified size and/or weight.

3. The model will have to have a function where they are aimed and activated, and they kick a model ball up and over a row of defending players.

4. You will get 3, 5, or 10 attempts to make the ball go over the defenders. If your player falls down, misses the ball during the kick, or breaks during an attempt, it is considered a failure.

5. You may have the opportunity to set up an offensive player that could deflect the ball into the goal past a stationary goalie for extra bonus points.

GRADED ASSIGNMENT SUGGESTIONS:

Grading suggestions include:

- a write-up of ideas, including blueprints

- grade results based upon the execution of the model and how accurately it reflects the proposed ideas

- a scoring sheet or infographic showing your kicking data

- a project about a corner kicks

MATERIALS:

INSTRUCTOR MATERIALS:

- Model soccer field or flat surface (a smooth table, a floor, fake turf, or sheet of melamine to make your rink on). Decorate your field and build a goal

- Scale models of nets and soccer balls

- Model goalkeeper and players (can be flat 2D printed reinforced images)

PARTICIPANT MATERIALS:

- paper clips

- notecards

- scissors

- plastic straws

- tape and glue

- popsicle sticks

- rubber bands and springs

- thread spools and string

- other approved materials

STANDARDS: ACCURACY, FORCES, MOTION, STATISTICS

Uniforms are a big part of any team in any sport. They're part psychology, part marketing, and part inspiration for a team. Design your own kit (uniform) for a soccer team, either fictional or real!

MISSION RULES AND RESTRICTIONS:

1. Research soccer kits (uniforms).

2. Use your research to help you design the perfect kit. Optionally, make alternate color schemes for away games.

3. Create a model of your kit idea. Your kit should include all of the major pieces: jersey, shorts, socks, footwear, and shin pads.

4. Also create an advertising scheme or sales pitch to present to your peers. Your presentation might include a pitch for a city that does not currently have a team.

5. Optionally, design a soccer field or stadium layout that reflects the team logo and theme.

MATERIALS:

INSTRUCTOR MATERIALS:

- student access to internet for research

- soccer kit examples

- optionally, miniature models or mannikins to place kits on.

PARTICIPANT MATERIALS:

- fabric, including athletic fabrics

- tape and glue

- colored tape

- paint

- sewing and design materials

- scissors

- other approved, scavenged materials

- access to printing for designs and logos

GRADED ASSIGNMENT SUGGESTIONS:

Grading suggestions include:

- a write-up of ideas, including blueprints

- grade results based upon the execution of the model and how accurately it reflects the proposed ideas

- a project about logos, team mascots, or a particular sports arena where soccer is played

| STANDARDS: | DESIGN, MATERIALS, MODELS |

| SOCCER: | GOAL CELEBRATIONS | |

Nothing is quite as fun as celebrating a goal. Choreograph your own goal celebration!

MISSION RULES AND RESTRICTIONS:

1. Watch examples of goal celebrations.
2. Create your own goal celebration.
3. Create a step-by-step plan of your celebration with stick figures, sketches, photographs, stop-motion animation, or other audio-visual elements.
4. Act out the goal celebration, especially (optionally) after scoring a goal on a field or on a mock-up of a goal.

MATERIALS:

INSTRUCTOR MATERIALS:

- student access to internet for research
- computers, cameras, and other available technology
- a space to set up a fake goal (optional)

PARTICIPANT MATERIALS:

- uniform (if possible)
- soccer ball
- a field to practice on
- art supplies to create your plan
- technology to create a plan

GRADED ASSIGNMENT SUGGESTIONS:

Grading suggestions include:

- a write-up of ideas, including blueprints
- an audio-visual highlights real of you as a fictitiously famous soccer player

| STANDARDS: | CHOREOGRAPHY, TECHNOLOGY |

SOCCER: ON THE PITCH

Soccer can't be played without a field, but what if it was different? What changes could you make to the field to change how it is played? Design your own field and/or stadium!

MISSION RULES AND RESTRICTIONS:

1. Research the design of a soccer field, paying special attention to the lines and zones of the pitch. Include research on how the game is played around those areas, such as the center circle, the penalty box, the goal area, and the midfield line.

2. Redesign soccer play, adding several new rules and modifications to the classic design of the lines and zones of the field. Position of lines, changes of dimensions, or added areas are some possible alterations.

3. Present your idea (with a model if possible).

4. If possible, play a game on a modified field (even at a smaller scale). This may be reserved for the game modification chosen as the best of the group.

GRADED ASSIGNMENT SUGGESTIONS:

Grading suggestions include:

• a write-up of ideas, including blueprints

• grade results based upon if the design actually works, and, if so, how successfully?

• a report on a soccer field, field surfaces and construction, or on the history of soccer field designs and rules

MATERIALS:

INSTRUCTOR MATERIALS:

• an actual soccer field if possible, or pictures of a real field

PARTICIPANT MATERIALS:

• poster board

• white melamine board

• access to printers

• colored tapes

• markers

• netting

• paint

• plastic straws

• foam sheeting

• cardboard

• fake turf carpet

STANDARDS: DESIGN, MATERIALS, MODELS

SOCCER: PENALTY KICKERS

One of the best scoring chances in soccer is the penalty kick. You get one after a defensive player commits a direct free kick offense in the penalty box. It's a 1-on-1 chance to go against the goalie. Make a model player that can kick a penalty kick!

MISSION RULES AND RESTRICTIONS:

1. Create a soccer player model of a specified size and/or weight.

2. The model will have to have a function where they are aimed and activated, and they kick the ball toward the net.

3. The soccer player will have to hit a ball about the size of a marble.

4. You will get 3, 5, or 10 attempts to make a goal. Missing the goal is a failure. Also, if your player falls down, misses the ball during the kick, or breaks during an attempt, it is considered a failure.

5. There will either be an active goalie or a stationary goalie at the time you shoot. Stationary goalies might be moved to a different defensive position prior to each shot.

GRADED ASSIGNMENT SUGGESTIONS:

Grading suggestions include:

- a write-up of ideas, including blueprints

- grade results based upon the execution of the model and how accurately it reflects the proposed ideas

- an infographic about penalties in soccer

- a project about a specific soccer goalkeeper or forward

MATERIALS:

INSTRUCTOR MATERIALS:

- Model soccer field or flat surface (a smooth table, a floor, fake turf, or sheet of melamine to make your rink on). Decorate your field and build a goal

- Scale models of nets and soccer balls

- Model goalkeeper

PARTICIPANT MATERIALS:

- paper clips

- notecards

- scissors

- plastic straws

- tape and glue

- popsicle sticks

- rubber bands and springs

- thread spools and string

- other approved materials

STANDARDS: ACCURACY, FORCES, MOTION, STATISTICS

SOCCER: SHOW STOPPERS

Without a goalie, the score of a soccer game would probably look like a football game. They're key for pacing the game, and for defense. Make your own goalkeeper model and practice blocking shots!

MISSION RULES AND RESTRICTIONS:

1. Create a soccer player model of a specified size and/or weight, which should include a full kit for realism, including gloves if possible.

2. The model will have to be controlled in front of the goal using a method of your choosing, which may include: puppetry, wind power, magnets, or another approved method.

3. The goalkeeper will have to stop a soccer ball about the size of a marble from going into a goal.

4. The goal will likely be built from pipe cleaners, plastic straws, and/or onion bag netting. It should be sized relative to the players.

5. You will get 3 to 10 shots to defend (multiple rounds may be required). If your goalie fails to stop the ball from going in the net, it is considered a goal.

GRADED ASSIGNMENT SUGGESTIONS:

Grading suggestions include:

• a write-up of ideas, including blueprints

• grade results based upon the execution of the model and how accurately it reflects the proposed ideas

• a project about a specific soccer goalie or the history of the goalie position and equipment in the sport

MATERIALS:

INSTRUCTOR MATERIALS:

• Model soccer field or flat surface (a smooth table, a floor, fake turf, or sheet of melamine to make your rink on). Decorate your field and build a goal

• Scale models of nets and soccer balls

PARTICIPANT MATERIALS:

• paper clips

• notecards

• scissors

• plastic straws

• tape and glue

• popsicle sticks

• foam

• brass fasteners

• string

• other approved materials

STANDARDS: ACCURACY, FORCES, FRICTION, MOTION, NEWTON'S LAWS

SOCCER: SLIDERS

One of the most dramatic defensive stops a player can make is a sliding tackle. This is when a defender slides and kicks the ball out of an opposing player's control (without drawing a penalty). Create a model of a sliding player.

MISSION RULES AND RESTRICTIONS:

1. Create a soccer player model of a specified size and/or weight, which could include a full kit for realism.

2. The model will have to have a function where they are aimed and activated, and they slide toward a model of a player with the ball.

3. Your sliding model should be able to accurately knock the ball away from the opposing player.

4. You will get 3 to 10 attempts to slide tackle. If your player fails to knock the ball away from the opposing player, it is a failure. If your player breaks, fails to activate, or misses entirely, it may be considered a failure as well.

MATERIALS:

INSTRUCTOR MATERIALS:

• Model soccer field or flat surface (a smooth table, a floor, fake turf, or sheet of melamine to make your rink on). Decorate your field and build a goal

• Scale models of players and soccer balls

PARTICIPANT MATERIALS:

• paper clips and clothespins

• notecards

• scissors

• plastic straws

• tape and glue

• popsicle sticks

• magnets

• rubber bands and springs

• thread spools and string

• other approved materials

GRADED ASSIGNMENT SUGGESTIONS:

Grading suggestions include:

• a write-up of ideas, including blueprints

• grade results based upon the execution of the model and how accurately it reflects the proposed ideas

• a project about a soccer defender or the positions in soccer

STANDARDS: ACCURACY, FORCES, FRICTION, MOTION

| SOCCER: | TABLE SOCCER TIME | |

Create your own table soccer game!

MISSION RULES AND RESTRICTIONS:

1. Look at the field of an actual soccer game.
2. Create a model version of the entire game that can be played on a table top. Your game could be a card game, a board game, or a moving part type game.
3. Create a set of rules.
4. Test play your game.
5. Optionally, create a sales pitch that would market your table top version of soccer.

MATERIALS:

INSTRUCTOR MATERIALS:

- pictures of actual foosball/ table soccer games (optional)

- samples of rules and other soccer materials

PARTICIPANT MATERIALS:

- plastic straws

- bamboo skewers

- tape and glue

- cardboard and boxes

- scissors

- markers and colors

- paper and card stock

- access to a printer

- other approved materials

GRADED ASSIGNMENT SUGGESTIONS:

Grading suggestions include:

- a write-up of ideas, including blueprints

- grade results based upon if the design actually works, and, if so, how successfully?

- a report on the history of soccer and major changes in rules and playing

| STANDARDS: | DESIGN, ENGINEERING, MEASUREMENT, MODELS |

| SOCCER: | TIME TO CLEAT | |

You can't play soccer very well with regular shoes. You need cleats. Soccer cleats are different from those used in baseball and golf. Design a set of cleats!

MISSION RULES AND RESTRICTIONS:

1. Research soccer cleats, as well as other types of cleats.
2. Use your research to help you design the perfect soccer cleat.
3. Create a model of your cleat idea.
4. Also create an advertising scheme or sales pitch to present to your peers.

MATERIALS:

INSTRUCTOR MATERIALS:

- student access to internet for research

- actual soccer cleats for comparison

PARTICIPANT MATERIALS:

- fabric, including heavier fabrics and rubber-type materials

- metal bands

- tape and glue

- rubber bands

- colored tape

- paint

- clay

- eyelets and shoelaces

- sewing and design materials

- scissors

- other approved, scavenged materials

GRADED ASSIGNMENT SUGGESTIONS:

Grading suggestions include:

- a write-up of ideas, including blueprints

- grade results based upon the execution of the model and how accurately it reflects the proposed ideas

- a report on cleats or a brand of cleats

- a project about feet and/or leg muscles

| STANDARDS: | ANATOMY, DESIGN, ERGONOMICS, MATERIALS, MODELS |

RESOURCE PAGES

* BLUEPRINTS * DATA * GRAPHING * REFLECTION * JOURNALS *

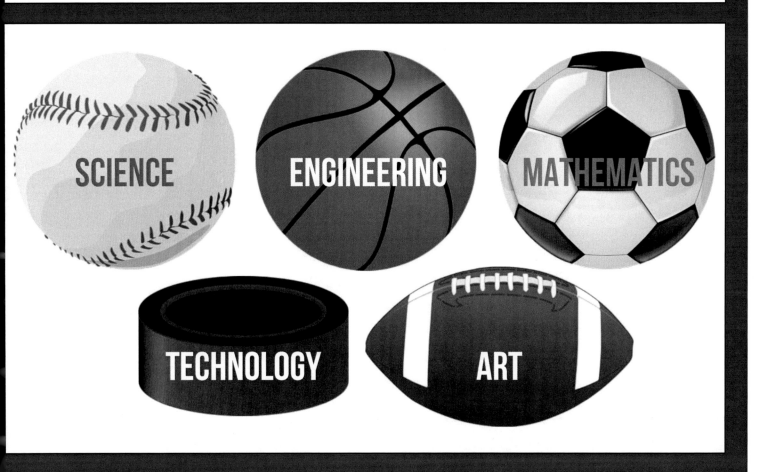

SCIENCE

ENGINEERING

MATHEMATICS

TECHNOLOGY

ART

MediaStream Press

JOURNALING SHEET

NAME:

WRITING AREA

PLANNING SHEET

NAME:

PLANNING AREA

BLUEPRINT SHEET

NAME:

DESIGN AREA

BLUEPRINT SHEET

NAME:

DESIGN AREA

DATA SHEET

NAME:

DATA RECORD AREA

DATA SHEET

NAME:

DATA RECORD AREA

OBSERVATIONS SHEET

NAME:

DRAWING & WRITING AREA

GRAPHING SHEET

SINGLE TRIAL DATA SHEET

DATA GRAPH

LEGEND

GRAPHING SHEET

MULTIPLE TRIAL DATA SHEET

TEST 1

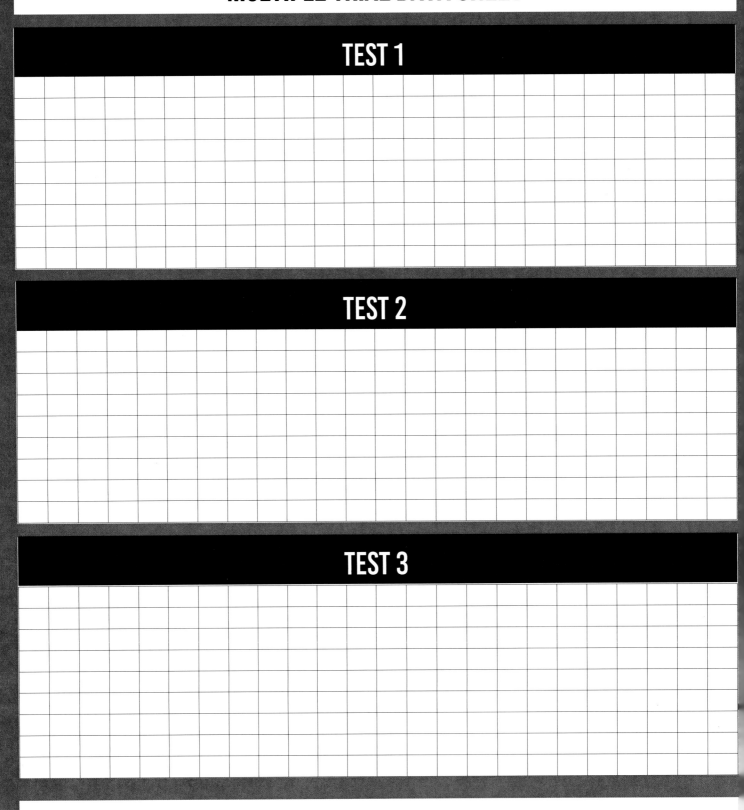

TEST 2

TEST 3

GRAPHING SHEET

MULTIPLE TRIAL DATA SHEET

TEST 1

TEST 2

TEST 3

ABOUT THE AUTHOR

ANDREW FRINKLE

ABOUT THE AUTHOR:

Andrew Frinkle is an award-nominated teacher and writer with experience in America and overseas, as well as years of developing educational materials for big name educational sites like Have Fun Teaching. He has taught PreK all the way up to adult classes, and has focused on ESOL/EFL techniques and STEM Education.

With two young children at home now, he's been developing more and more teaching strategies and books aimed at helping young learners, as well as games and activity books for primary grades.

Andrew Frinkle is the founder & owner of MediaStream Press LLC. He also writes fantasy and science fiction novels under the pen name Velerion Damarke and writes/illustrates children's fiction as Andrew Frinkle. Additionally, he is working on educational music albums.

CONTACT INFORMATION:

MediaStream Press currently operates and maintains the following sites:
www.MediaStreamPress.com
- www.50STEMLabs.com
- www.AndrewFrinkle.com
- www.common-core-assessments.com
- www.littlelearninglabs.com
- www.underspace.org

Purchase his books and educational materials from one of the following sites:
www.amazon.com/author/andrewfrinkle/
www.amazon.com/author/veleriondamarke/
www.teacherspayteachers.com/Store/Velerion-Damarke

MEDIASTREAM PRESS

BOOKS, GAMES, & MEDIA

WWW.MEDIASTREAMPRESS.COM

ALSO ON:

WWW.TEACHERSPAYTEACHERS.COM/STORE/VELERION-DAMARKE

50 STEM LABS

ACTIVITIES FOR STEM, STEAM, AND ENGINEERING

WWW.50STEMLABS.COM

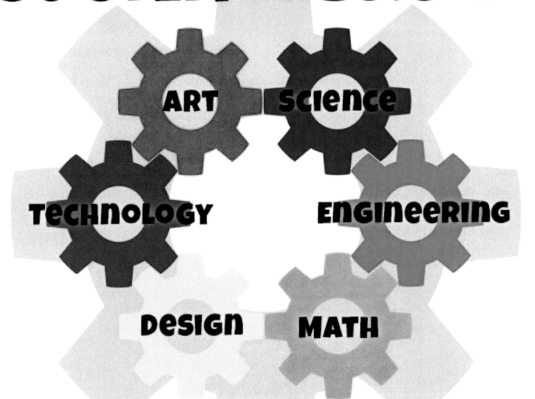

ALSO ON:

WWW.TEACHERSPAYTEACHERS.COM/STORE/VELERION-DAMARKE

Made in the USA
Las Vegas, NV
30 October 2022

58453628R00048